LECTURES ON ORGANIZATION

DELIVERED IN THE COURSE ON INDUSTRIAL ORGANIZATION IN THE GRADUATE SCHOOL OF BUSINESS ADMINISTRATION OF HARVARD UNIVERSITY

BY

RUSSELL ROBB, 1864-

Privately Printed

COPYRIGHT, 1910, BY RUSSELL ROBB

ALL RIGHTS RESERVED

CONTENTS

ORGANIZATION AS AFFECTED BY PURPOSE AND CONDITIONS 1

THE LIMITS OF ORGANIZATION 24

THE ORGANIZATION OF ADMINISTRATION 47

ORGANIZATION AS AFFECTED BY PURPOSE AND CONDITIONS

As an industry or business begins to involve large size, great numbers, and complexity, organization becomes necessary simply for the direction, control, and handling of affairs, quite aside from any question of direct economy. It becomes necessary to set off groups of workers, to divide responsibilities, duties, and processes, so that affairs may be kept within the scope and ability of those who are directing the undertaking. A virtue has, however, been made of this necessity for division, because it becomes possible, by dividing duties and functions, to conserve special skill, ability, and use, and to direct all effort into definite paths, to which it becomes accustomed and thus gains in efficiency.

It is of little importance how the great growth in industries has come, — whether a realization of the benefits that arise with division of labor and conserving of skill induced us to gain size so that these advantages might be brought into play, or whether size came first and the advantages were a fortuitous accompaniment. It seems, however, to be true in most cases that the need for having matters more thoroughly in hand, the need for better command of affairs by administrative officers, usually results in a division that makes plainer the lines of authority, that places responsibility more definitely, and secures discipline, while in the consideration of the economies to be secured in the different parts of the organization, attention is more often given to questions of division of duties to secure specialization in skill and plant, to the limiting of duties to functions instead of parts only.

If, for instance, one were suddenly required to organize a body of thousands of men to clear the streets of a city from an abnormally heavy fall of snow, it is probable that these men would be divided into divisions, each with a chief, and that these divisions would be divided into squads, each with a foreman. The division would be divided into similar kinds of units, headed by men in absolute authority over their units and with no collateral relations to cause complications and delay. The organization would be for the purpose of control, for the purpose of intimate command and effective direction. If, however, one were to organize a great industrial establishment to manufacture machines that had very close competition both as to quality and price, the greatest care would have to be given in the organization to the different functions in the manufacture, and to the segregation of such functions as designing, purchasing, and selling, so that every advantage could be taken of special knowledge and specialization of effort.

Other activities that are not industrial, such as the church, the civil government, the army, the navy, educational organizations, charitable organizations, all involve size and numbers and complexity, and they are all organized; but good industrial organization will be likely to differ from these other organizations, and all organizations will differ somewhat from each other, because the objects, the results that are sought, and the way these results must be attained, are different; and, moreover, the material out of which the organization is made, differs in kind.

It is, of course, true that there is much that is common to all effective endeavor: the definite knowledge of what one wishes to accomplish; the principles of directing and controlling effectively large numbers of people; making the most of different kinds of skill; the securing of coöperation, so that each one helps instead of hinders another; the systematic and orderly way of doing things, so that there are no neglected steps, no false movements, no lost time — are all common to good organizations of all kinds. But, with differing purposes, the factors that make organization have varying importance. With one purpose in view, the principle of the division of labor for specialization of skill may be all-important; in another situation, this may become insignificant in comparison with the proper control and direction of large numbers. The problem in another organization may be the systematization and division of work mainly to bring order and efficiency into a situation of complexity. The significant feature in another case may be almost wholly a question of dispatch, where the question of economy even may hinge much more on the time required than on any other factor. Again, we may have success hinging upon systems of accounting, records, and statistics, where the accurate knowledge of costs and other details of the business, and the system for securing these, may be the central factor about which the organization is constructed.

It is interesting to consider some of the different forms that organizations take and some of the results that are sought, because such a consideration brings out more clearly this question of purpose and conditions and material, and helps to prevent one from assuming that organization always means the application of a perfectly definite method or system to the carrying out of any large and complicated undertaking.

In the popular mind, perfect organization usually is associated with the army. The division of the men into companies and regiments, the clearly defined duties and authority of the officers, the discipline that secures precision in all evolutions and obedience to all commands of the superiors, suggest to most people the perfection of concerted action, and furnish the type to which they feel that all organizations should conform as nearly as possible. And so, when they see that an industrial establishment is large, they speak of its members as an "industrial army" and its head as a "captain of industry." The regularity of hours in an organized industry, the definite and formal orders, and the established lines of authority, all suggest to us that very old type of organization that has had for its purpose the handling of large numbers of men in fighting. An army in modern times, with its different branches of service, its attention to commissary and sanitation, its great multiplicity of technical appliances of war, its connection with the activities of civil life, becomes very complex; but in the beginning, military organization was a necessity in order to direct and handle effectively large numbers of men, and so to prevent the hordes who went fighting from being merely a mob. The great numbers acting together could not act effectively unless there were order and system in all their evolutions, and an organization binding the order and system together. Moreover, the product came in one supreme moment: the organization was for an emergency. Its whole success or failure was shown by the action of the army at a critical time; and for this reason military organization has taken a severe line, in which everything is subordinated to obedience and definiteness of procedure and certainty of predetermined evolution and action upon command. Authority and responsibility taper down with evenness, each one knowing his exact limitations and his part. Each one in authority must be trained to assume instantly all the duties of the one next above, for the captain of one moment may be colonel in the next.

Military organization has contributed much to all

other types of organization through its example of the value of discipline, the usefulness of definite procedure, and the effectiveness in administration of placing responsibility, but it has been the cause of mistakes in building up other organizations, through the forcing into prominence of the main features of a military organization when the end that is sought is much more influenced by other factors, when the necessity for control is less than for specialization of effort and for the coördination of different kinds of action. This becomes plainer when one considers, for instance, an industrial organization depending for its success very largely upon the ability with which the principles of division of labor are applied. There are many examples. Take the making of watches. Here we have great numbers working together, but they are not interchangeable units, nor are those who direct the workers interchangeable and in direct line of authority. There are numberless processes, in each of which workers are trained and practiced until their skill vastly exceeds that of a novice. There are large numbers of different machines, — processes are divided and subdivided and simplified, to attain the acme of the worker's deftness, and to sift from his duties all but the one in which he is supreme. The military virtues here are still desirable to an extent, but they are only incidental. They are not the factors that determine whether good watches are or are not to be turned out at a low cost. The success or failure of the watch-industry would not depend upon instant obedience, upon definite evolutions of men, upon predetermined movement in emergency, upon a definite line of succession in authority, it would depend upon such things as study and care and economy in purchasing materials, upon the development of processes to make the most of each worker's special skill and ability, the saving of time in the handling of the product, the working of the plant to save interest and rent, the discovery of consumers, and the prompt delivery of the product. The main purpose is different from the main military purpose, and the organization must vary accordingly.

Large and complex construction is often undertaken where, in the words of contracts, " time is of the essence." The need for the structure may be vital to the integrity of an important business already established. The saving in interest and in earning power, if the work is completed in months instead of in a year or two, may be a large amount. The organization for such an undertaking will not be the same as for deliberate construction systematized in all details for the lowest total construction-cost. It may be necessary to cut " red tape " that would be desirable in other situations, it may pay to take the chances of less thorough deliberation of plans, the lines of authority even may be changed, — all because the relative importance of factors is changed. The harmony of the organization is upset, and modifications must be made to suit the new conditions.

This was shown two years ago when the Boston

Elevated Railway Company discovered that it must have very large additions to three different power-stations in order to care properly for its maximum load the following Christmas. There were but twelve months in which to design and build the stations. The organization of a street railway could not economically provide for emergency construction of such magnitude, and even the engineering company that did the work found it necessary to make important modifications in its organization in order to secure dispatch, even at the risk of losing the greatest economy in all details. It was necessary to place as much responsibility down along the line as possible, so that time would not be lost in referring questions for confirmation. It was necessary that the work be segregated, so that in functional departments there would be no question of "right of way." The specialization was in the direction of "Boston Elevated work," not in the direction of "electrical engineering," or "purchasing," or "drafting." A special smaller organization was set off for this particular piece of work. The construction manager in charge had complete authority over it, except as he was responsible to the president of the engineering company. He had under him three assistant construction managers, each of whom was responsible for one of the stations. Each of these assistants had a night and day engineer in charge of the actual construction. Each station had its own inspectors and its own survey corps. The special organization for this work had its own draftsmen and its own purchasing department and its own accounting department. There was no attempt to serve it from the functional departments of the engineering company organization. Every endeavor was to secure short-cuts in time. The stations were operating in ten months from the time they were begun, and ordinarily it had taken a year and a half or two years to accomplish the same thing. This was an organization for dispatch, — to get a piece of work done in order to save the expense of delay, which would have greatly overbalanced any economy there might have been in a less military but more functional form of organization.

The construction of the great irrigating reservoirs in India, where a few years ago during the famine so many of the natives were employed, furnishes a good example of the variation in organizations according to the material one has to work with. One can imagine approximately what sort of an organization would be necessary in most other places to undertake the vast excavations necessary to form reservoirs in great irrigating works: there would be a large mechanical equipment of steam-shovels, with the minor organization of drivers, mechanicians, and superintendents, the systems of records, of fuel-supply and repairs; the placing of equipment; the orderly procedure of the work; the great number of workmen to direct and supervise; the systems of pay, shelter, commissary, sanitation, — all would have to be moulded into a great comprehensive organization.

In India there were no steam-shovels, mechanicians, fuel-supply, repairs, shelters, or commissary. The excavation was done directly by hordes of natives in gangs of twenty or thirty, each with his or her basket, and one with his little " scooper " or koiti. When the basket was filled, it went on the worker's head and was carried to the dump, where the native received a small tag that entitled him to payment for one basketful of excavation. The workers consisted of gangs, over which were the foremen who furnished the laborers for the work. There was no system of housing, for there were no shelters : all slept on the ground in the open. There was no commissary organization, for the workers "found themselves," and in any case would have refused any food prepared for them, because of caste prejudice. The payment of workers required no elaborate system of pay-rolls and receipts, because each worker simply cashed in the tags he had received. No doubt those in charge of these Indian excavations had their problems of organization, but they were different from our problems, and probably the most of our approved systems would have been of about as much use as an American typewriter to a Chinese merchant.

There are all kinds of industries, and one is perhaps as good as another for the purpose of illustrating organization. If one is credibly informed, the organization of some of the patent-medicine companies differs considerably from that of other manufacturing companies, and yet they are still ably organized. There is at least one where two or three rooms in a large building are devoted to the manufacture of the medicine, a minor function in the organization. The remainder of the building is largely devoted to a printing establishment for the preparation of advertising matter, to advertising departments, correspondence-clerks, and stenographers. Here we have a manufacturing establishment, but the purpose and conditions require special attention to the office-system. The accomplishment of the purpose is not greatly affected by attention to manufacturing methods and details, but is very greatly affected by skill in advertisement and system in the departments where the real effort and most of the expense lie.

Four or five in particular of the insurance companies learned at the time of the Chelsea fire to appreciate the importance in their organizations of complete and systematic records, and will doubtless have increased respect for this factor in their organizations. As soon as it became known that the conflagration would be wide-spread and cause great loss, one of the insurance companies card-indexed all its risks in the burned district. From their records they were able to set down at once the different companies that were interested in the insurance, and what the amounts of their risks were. Four or five of the companies coöperated, all necessary information was compiled, and members of the group were able to write each policy-holder within a day or two that the companies were ready to make appointments with the insured and the adjustment-bureau, and settle claims. The satisfaction of the insured may well be imagined, for the ordinary procedure would have required about a month; thus the efficient recording systems proved their great value, not only as an adjunct in office-system, but as a very important factor in the relations between the company and those with whom it did business.

There has grown up in this country of late years a new form of business organization that is of interest in this consideration of different purposes and material. This is the organization for the selling of negotiable securities, principally bonds to investors. The larger bond houses have a very large number of salesmen,—a number large enough to suggest in a manufacturing establishment division of labor, lines of authority, systems of time-keeping, and other approved principles for the securing of good and economical work. But these particular principles of organization in a bond house sink to a very subordinate place. These salesmen are very nearly independent units; many of them have their own clients; they will have their own ways of finding, meeting, and convincing investors. Organization here takes a different line: it is in the direction of systematic buying of securities suitable to offer to purchasers, of acquainting the men with the principles of the house, the systematic presentation to them of the merits of the security they are to sell, the card-indexing of customers, records of transactions, dissemination of information, canvassing of fields; but not very much thought about the principles of division of labor or of the military virtues.

Most organizations have grown gradually, and the conditions surrounding this growth often influence greatly the form that the final organization takes. Long existence of customs and methods, and the consequent knowledge of the plan throughout the organization, may be of more importance than the features that might be secured by a theoretically better structure. It is understood, for instance, that the very successful Studebaker organization is administered by an executive committee of five members, each member of which is at the head of a functional department of the business. Committees are not ordinarily very effective as heads of undertakings. They have difficulty in reaching decisions, and one member is likely to prove dominant and carry his ideas without being responsible for the results. The Studebaker organization, however, has grown up about a family of five brothers, all able and active in the business. From small beginnings they had threshed out their problems together and had learned the art of conference. They had found how to draw from each his contribution to the general knowledge and to the particular question, and they had discovered ways of reaching conclusions without interminable discussions or unplaced responsibility. One might hesitate to form a new organization on this plan, but he would just as surely fail to discard it, when so completely established and so well proved in efficiency. In parts, at least, of many organizations, one finds variations from the theoretically best plan on account of the personality or particular ability of important officers or heads. The individual ordinarily has small influence on the general plan of very large organizations, but in the lesser ones the failure to benefit from exceptional ability in broad grasp and direction, or the failure to make the most of unusual knowledge and skill in special directions, may lose to the undertaking far more than the seemingly perfect structure could secure.

It will be unfortunate if the emphasis given here to the diversity of conditions and to the difference in the purposes of undertakings should be construed as an argument that no general principles can be applied to organization. It is intended simply to show that there is no "royal road," no formula that, once learned, may be applied in all cases with the assurance that the result will be perfect harmony, efficiency, and economy, and a sure path to the main purpose in view. This is not an imagined difficulty. We all are inclined to get a bit twisted toward some favorite panacea, and if one is to attempt to better a business organization, it helps greatly to be able to approach the problem with an open mind, and not to have a special predilection toward a factor that one has somewhere found admirable. One sees frequently men who are biased in favor of military organization, — they have admired the precision, the definiteness, and the well-defined authority and responsibility, and once enamored, they would apply it indiscriminately. Another man in his experience has seen kinds of work clearly defined and important in their functions, and has been impressed with special skill. He becomes twisted toward specialization, and would apply " functional organization " everywhere, often regardless of the advantages of clearly defined responsibility for results as a whole. Now and then when a man discovers in his business some remarkable facts, through the medium of records and statistics, he begins to look upon these as embodying real organization, and this may become one of the most fatal of twists, because of possible records and statistics there is no end. It is one of the important factors in organization because it has to do with the very first principles, — our knowledge of what we are accomplishing and can accomplish; but in an organization for doing things, this gathering of knowledge has its limits, — in organizations of some kinds it has narrow limits, and our enthusiast for records and statistics becomes sometimes like the perennial student, who absorbs during all his life and never produces.

There has been a tremendous advance in the last generation in " system." So great has been the improvement in the method and order with which business of all kinds is conducted, and so important is it in the prevention of waste, that we find many who look upon the systematic doing of things as organization itself. And so it is nearly the whole of organization in some cases; but it is easy here to fall into thinking that a system that saves much in one organization is a universal factor, and will be just as effectual wherever applied. An illustration of this is a detail in the letter-filing system of a certain business house. The needs of this particular business often require that letters be referred to several different departments, that notations or remarks be made by one or more department heads, and sometimes that letters be retained by a department pending investigation. It was found that notations were often so many that a special tag attached to the letter was advisable, and moreover that letters were often missing from the files when wanted, and it was necessary to search many departments to find them. There was danger of important letters being lost altogether in their wanderings. The difficulties are met by pasting on each letter as it is received a tag about four inches by five. On this tag is stamped the time when it is received, a serial number, the department to which it is referred, spaces for remarks, and spaces for noting date of answer and date of filing. In a record-book is entered by the mailing department the date and serial number of every letter as received, the department to which it is referred, and the number of the correspondent. Every letter that is referred from one department

BY PURPOSE AND CONDITIONS

to another is taken by a mailing-department boy, and the change is noted on the record-book. In this way there is a record of every letter, who has had it, and where it is. This all, of course, is a detail in a system, but in the particular organization where it is used, it is an important detail and has saved a tremendous amount of the time of the head men directly and indirectly, as well as furnishing assurance that important letters can always be placed when wanted. Now, in certainly nine out of ten organizations this system of recording letters would be an over-elaboration. It would be a needless expense, and would often clog rather than lubricate the machinery of business; yet if one of the mail-clerks brought up in this system were called upon to systematize a mailing department in another organization, it would be perfectly natural for him to base his system on the one that he knew had proved a good one.

Yet, in spite of the wide differences in organizations, we do, to use a mathematical term, know the "dimensions" of organization. We do know the quantities which, of some magnitude or other, according to purposes and conditions, are the component parts.

We can conceive of no real organization, for instance, without a structure of some kind, without a definite plan. However work is apportioned, and by whatever means it is directed and carried out, we may be sure that the method must have definiteness. We may choose the wrong kind of men to do things, we may not plan to bring their work to them so that their time is most efficiently used, we may not use care that special skill is conserved; but if we have some plan that assigns definite duties, if we have some order by which all the necessary action is taken, we have made a beginning in organization.

We have, too, from our earlier organizations, the examples of the value of lines of authority. They add to definiteness. They provide the control and direction by subdividing for that purpose. As authority tapers down, it relieves from responsibility except in the fields for which men are fitted. It provides a definite court of appeal in case of difficulty, and thus saves endless disputes and arguments and consequent confusion. This tapering authority never leaves affairs without a head, and it assures the steady progress of the undertaking because it provides a properly trained supply of new men to fill vacated superior positions.

We know also the value of the factor of responsibility in organization, the great incentive there is to careful and energetic work when praise and blame can be accurately placed, and we know that, as this responsibility is segregated, as men are relieved from divided responsibility, initiative increases, and we get the vigor of independent action and leave ability untrammeled.

As undertakings become more complex, the factor of division of labor, of specialization, grows in importance. We use great care in choosing men for their different duties according to their fitness, and we increase this fitness and create special skill by narrowing duties so that all attention and study and practice are confined in one direction. In division of labor, advantage is taken of a natural tendency. Men do most readily what they can do best. It increases their interest and enthusiasm and efficiency.

We know that a great factor in organization is "system," the mechanism of the whole. It transmits intellectual power, physical power, and skill to the main purpose. It touches all parts of the undertaking, for it is the introduction everywhere of order and method. It relieves those who direct from the details of execution, and it relieves the man with special skill from the duties for which he is less well fitted. It brings work to men in condition for the application of their particular function. It moves all in accustomed routine so that the waste involved in initial effort is avoided. It insures that important steps will not be forgotten. It makes use of mechanical aids to save human labor and thought. It arranges the processes so that the greatest good is secured from the use of the property devoted to the undertaking, and it introduces method into the use, so that the property is not idle, — so that time, the opportunity for accomplishment, is not wasted.

With system and order, the value of discipline appears as a factor, for it holds all to the chosen system of working. It has to do with the rules and regulations necessary to carry out the system, with securing obedience to these rules, and with the training and instruction that assures full understanding. As a part of the maintaining of the system, is the provision for watchfulness and supervision to keep the movement in the right direction, and the provision for checks to insure against dishonesty, against errors in judgment, and errors from carelessness.

We have another very important factor in organization, in accounting, records, and statistics, for these furnish the chart and the compass, the sounding-lead and the log. They are to show us where we are, where we have come from, where we are tending and how fast, and where the shoals lie, and they can tell us, too, how the craft is working. They must be largely depended upon to acquaint those who are directing undertakings with the progress and with the conditions, and this becomes more marked as organizations become larger and more complex, because it becomes increasingly difficult for those at the top to gather their knowledge from their own observation. It is not only from lack of time to observe that this is so, but in the complexity of modern organizations a great amount of analysis is necessary, simply to segregate information, so that a problem may be clearly presented. One hears less in these days of the successful and shrewd old men of affairs who kept little more than memorandum-books and had all the detail of their business in their heads; that was a possibility in competing with

BY PURPOSE AND CONDITIONS 21

lesser men doing the same thing, and in a time when the product of even a very rough organization was worth much more than the cost of all that went into it. Modern industrial organizations are by no means wholly a fortunate development that widens the difference between cost and value of product. They are also born of necessity to save a margin growing smaller; and when one has to do with disappearing margins he can no longer depend upon inclinations and rough judgments. He has to deal with figures, and his system of figures must represent the true state of affairs. Naturally enough, it is here that one usually finds the greatest difference between industrial organizations and other organizations, because it is the price of the life of an industry, — this knowledge of exactly what is being accomplished and what it is costing to accomplish it.

An organization is much looked upon as a machine, as a cold-blooded product of synthesis, as an artificial sort of being that recognizes such realities as order, system, discipline, skill, and ability, but has no place anywhere for the "spirit" of anything. But if we are to look upon "organization" as something more than "system," if it is to be a sort of organism, we must recognize another factor, and that is *esprit de corps*. It induces enthusiastic and unselfish working together, with regard more to the whole result than immediately to one's own personal part in the achievement. It leads one to do his part well for the advancement of the whole. It leads one to see the advancement in his part because the whole is gaining in achievement and stability. If we have the military groups, it makes those groups support one another and act together as one; if we have the functional groups, it removes the friction, it covers the borderland, it helps to coördinate. It is not easy to define this spirit exactly. It is not mechanical and is not obtainable on command, but it gives life and power to the organization. It will not exist without some understanding of the whole and without respect for the purpose and methods. It comes down from the top. It is a reflection of the feeling and the policy of those directing, a reflection of the respect of the superiors for their purpose, and of their earnestness in their work, and of their feeling toward those farther down who are joining in the work. It is a spirit of the whole, and cannot exist without consideration of the units. Organizations are not difficult to sketch out on paper. They always have there a definite and workable look, as if nothing could escape a far-reaching arm that would pull all into the hopper somewhere; but in the working organization, unless it be the most simple, there is constant call for the unscheduled coöperation, for the action that can be secured only through a genuine, lively, and loyal interest in the success of the whole undertaking. And it is interesting here to note that this sort of thing is often expressed by a simile that is the outcome of the activities of intercollegiate life, for we urge this spirit by urging "team play."

Thus, we know pretty definitely the factors that make organization. They are structure, lines of authority, responsibility, division of labor, system, discipline; accounting, records, and statistics; and *esprit de corps*, coöperation, "team play"; but when we attempt to determine the parts played by these factors, we find that their relative importance changes with purpose, conditions, and material. We begin to realize that there is an art of organizing that requires knowledge of aims, processes, men, and conditions, as well as of the principles of organization.

THE LIMITS OF ORGANIZATION

THE gain from organization is so evident when it is applied to a confused situation, and the satisfaction so great in having affairs run smoothly, that, as we continue grouping forces and introducing system, we easily become convinced that we cannot have too much of it. Like the "diminishing returns in agriculture," however, the returns from increasing organization do not continue proportional to the effort, and limits are reached, beyond which one may well proceed with care. It becomes necessary sometimes to remind ourselves that organization, as an end in itself, is of no value. A business organization is for the purpose of accomplishing definite pieces of work, of arriving at a definite result with the least expenditure of labor and material, the smallest expenditure for plant, and the shortest time of use of the plant; and if organization does not prevent waste or enable us to get results attainable in no other way, it has no value.

To increase the efficiency of effort, we must go beyond the perfection of the organization machinery as machinery: we must know in what directions effort will yield the greatest returns, which factors in a result have the greatest bearing and will best repay study and attention, which items are unimportant and the last that should have consideration.

Many years ago there was a course of study at the Institute of Technology that was purely a technical course for the benefit of engineering students in their professional work. The subject of the course was "The Precision of Measurements," and it may be assumed that it was not intended to be specially helpful in practical business; and yet to those of us who were interested and were impressed with the principles that were established, this course went much farther than to furnish a sound method in physical measurement — it was found to be broadly applicable to much other work, and even suggested to many of us a basis for a philosophy of effective endeavor.

The principles emphasized were that most final results are not single measurements, but are the results of the combination of several quantities of different kinds and of a more or less complex computation; that the measurement of energy, for instance, in foot-pounds, would involve the combination of measurements of distance and weight, and that the measurement of the work done upon one side of the piston of an engine in one stroke, as another instance, would involve the combination of measurements of diameter of piston, the mean intensity of pressure, the length of stroke, and would also involve a more or less precise value of π. It would not be possible to have perfection in these measurements, and the accuracy with which the different components could be determined would vary greatly. In measuring the work done upon the piston, it would be easy to get a pretty accurate measurement of the diameter of piston and length of stroke, but the pressure is difficult to measure, and the accuracy would be much less than with piston and stroke-measurements, and of course far less than the accuracy of the value of π, which can be carried out as many places as desired. Moreover, it also appears that for the best precision in the final result it will be worth while to measure the diameter of piston more carefully than the length of stroke, because in the final result the diameter is squared, and is thus a factor of greater importance. It also was proved to us that nothing was gained in precision by carrying out the value of π to a great many places, or by measuring the length of stroke as accurately as we could, because in any case the influence in the final results of the rather rough measurement of pressure would entirely overshadow the refinements in the accuracy of the other components; that the really significant figures in the value of π, for instance, would in the example given be very few, and after four or five places would be insignificant.

We were taught to lay out our problem in advance, to learn before we began that we must measure length and diameter and pressure, and to determine in advance what influence each of these factors had in the result. We were urged to learn our limitations in the determination of each of these different factors, so that we should not waste time in fruitless refinement, or end with a false idea of the precision of the result. This seems a perfectly obvious procedure, that the exercise of common sense would always lead us to follow; but in reality we are not likely to follow it unless we make a studied attempt to do so. When we know that we have to measure factors like length of stroke or diameter of piston, there is a tendency to go straight to work at them; and if we pride ourselves on being thorough, we devise ultra precise methods to get as near perfection as we can before we pass to the next factor. When we get to the determination of pressure, we discover that no precise measure is possible, and that the bearing of this factor on the whole result is such that we might just as well have rested content with approximate and easy measurements of our linear quantities. We are so constituted, however, that we cannot help a virtuous feeling when we contemplate our length-standards corrected for temperature and our micrometer adjustments arranged with such painstaking care. We pride ourselves that at any rate we have done the best we can, and have a lot of work carried out systematically to show for it. Yet all but two minutes of it was worth nothing whatever.

It is very easy to fall into this way of doing things. A year or two ago the price of copper-wire was in a very unstable position. It had been selling unusually high, and then began dropping a quarter and a half cent a pound in a few days. No one knew whether he would have to pay in a month's time twenty cents or fifteen cents a pound, and yet in some of the estimates of the period one would be likely to find results predicated on the existing market price, — he would find elaborate calculations to show the advisable type of electrical machinery to use in a given case when the dominating factor was changing so fast that no one could determine the result within a wide range of probability. Such estimates were not an example of accurate and praiseworthy work. They were unmeaning and foolish. They produced only insignificant figures, because the variation in an important factor was overwhelming in its influence.

Within the memory of all of us, the bicycle industry was exceedingly profitable and growing like a weed. There seemed no limit to the possible output of factories. The manufacture involved many parts and processes, and involved much special skill. Every bicycle manufacturer could see that thorough organization of his business would result in better product at lower production-cost. Some of the manufacturers introduced all approved methods, enlarged the scope of their concerns to include practically all of the parts of the complete machine. They built substantial and elaborate plants that the investigations of specialists and the calculations of engineers showed were best adapted for the work. Much of this organization was admirable and justified. If any of us had been asked at this time which establishment

THE LIMITS OF ORGANIZATION 29

had the best organization, we should doubtless have picked out one of the very complete ones, one with model and substantial factories, but we should very likely have been wrong, because it was proved in very few years that the organization that happened to have in its administrative staff a good student in human nature, an expert on the stability of fads and fancies, was the one that had the really effective organization. The great activity in the industry was short-lived. Those who realized that it probably would be short-lived, organized as well as they could for the operating expenses, but they were wary about large permanent investments, for these required many years of successful business to justify them. One of the most important factors in the business was the time it was to last, and some apparently gave it little thought.

Some of this may sound rather technical and not specially applicable to business organization, and some of it may seem perfectly obvious, but it brings out some general principles in the attainment of any result, which we may know perfectly well, but which we often fail to apply with any care. It makes us realize more clearly that in every problem there are many factors — in any undertaking there are many things that influence the result; that we shall make the best use of time, labor, and money if we keep all these factors in view, if we develop the whole in harmony, consider the bearing of the factors, and work for their improvement in proportion to their influence, instead of getting twists in one direction because it happens to interest us or is easy of progress, or because it is in plain view. It helps us to an appreciation of the true kind of thoroughness, of the value of attention to what is significant, and the elimination as a waste of time and effort of what in our "Precision of Measurements" was represented by the insignificant figures. It saves us from seeking too great a degree of perfection in a detail because it teaches us that perfection in one detail may add only in an infinitesimal degree to probable perfection in the whole.

This question of thoroughness is well illustrated by an example furnished by an Institute of Technology graduate some twenty years ago. At that time it was rather the fashion for electrical engineers to go upon graduation to the factories of the Thomson-Houston Electric Company at Lynn, Mass. They entered there what was called the Expert Department. The company at that time was much in need of trained men to superintend the installation of electric plants, and in order to give these men a fairly comprehensive idea of electric construction, the Electric Company arranged an expert course to last two or three years. During this time the technical-school graduates spent a little time in all important branches of the factory work, getting in this way not detailed knowledge of manufacturing, but a fairly complete idea of all the factors that made up a sufficient knowledge of plant-construction. They learned something about electric-wiring, about winding armatures, tested the different types of machines, learned about their adjustment, and gained some familiarity with all branches of the business as it was then constituted. One of the Institute graduates who went to Lynn was not at all satisfied with this method. He thought that it resulted in a superficial smattering of knowledge about a great many things, and it did not at all suit his earnest and conscientious way of going about things. He decided that he would do differently, because he wanted to know the details; so he obtained permission to take a different sort of course of his own. Rheostats, or resistance-boxes, were considered pretty important pieces of apparatus in those days, and he thought that a good place to begin was in the rheostat department, where he intended to stay long enough to know thoroughly every item of the construction, so that if at any time it became necessary for him to make a rheostat, or know what the matter was with a defective one, he would have the most intimate knowledge of its construction. He accordingly set off six months for this work and spent his six months building rheostats. He had just about finished his time when the company decided it would change the type of rheostat, and they were thereafter built after an entirely different design. This man's whole six months' work had gone for nothing except for such incidental experience as he obtained.

It is dangerous to criticise old sayings, they usually have so much truth in them, but one wishes that the familiar saying, "It is the little things that count," were not quite so short and were more specific, for it is responsible for much of this wrong kind of thoroughness. No one would contend, of course, that a multitude of little things do not in the aggregate amount to much, and there usually comes a time when every detail must in its turn be studied. But there is always the same old problem, "how many significant figures?" how far is it worth while to go in accuracy of detail in connection with one factor before one is sure he has taken into account all factors? Certainly in a business organization one is likely to reach better results if he first makes sure that all the factors are taken into account, and that endeavor is toward coördination and a real organism, than he will if his mind is down close to detail before the general plan and method are determined.

One sees often this close attention to very perfect systematization in departments of a business, and at the same time very little attention to some factor that is overwhelming in its importance. A few years ago a manufacturing concern had some difficulty in making a profit from its products, and to determine the cost more accurately, it established a very complete system of shop-cost records, so that it might be known which products were causing a loss. Much time and care were given to the accurate determination of all factors that entered into the shop-cost. A period of trial showed various margins in the different classes. The overhead costs, the general expenses, administration, and selling were known to be high for the amount of business, and a larger business was depended upon to correct this ; but it was only some time later that it was discovered that one of the classes of products showing a very good shop-margin was costing so much in general expense and cost of selling that there was no hope of ever making a profit, regardless of the perfection of shop-organization alone. Certainly in business organization, fully as much respect must be accorded the old warning about " saving at the spigot and wasting at the bunghole" as we accord to the saying, "It is the little things that count."

Now and then there are men who seem to go at once to the root of a question, and who, from a mass of detailed explanation, exposition, and talk, seem suddenly to pick from the medley the two or three salient features, — the things of such transcendent importance that all else drops away as if mere comment. Such men have a proper sense of proportion and the true sense of thoroughness, because they do not get involved in detail before they have blocked out the plan.

When it is urged that it is not worth while to follow all detail in every direction, when it is urged that one must first make sure that he knows in which direction it is most profitable, in a broad sense, to work, this must not be mistaken as advising a policy of " good enough," for it is not that; it is the policy of refusing to waste our resources on the non-essential and the ineffectual; it is being dissatisfied with the accomplishment of the infinitesimal in one direction when accomplishment of magnitude is possible in another; it is refusing to be like the man who thinks he is progressing through space when he walks forward in a train that is backing up at forty miles an hour. It is not to get short cuts and save work, but to make effective work, to expend the time and energy where it will accomplish the most. With an individual, so much depends upon his peculiar abilities and upon the interest and enthusiasm that he brings to any work, that there is less opportunity perhaps for choosing the lines of effort that appear upon cold analysis to be most essential to the forwarding of a result; but as work becomes more complex, as greater numbers coöperate to carry out undertakings, as we mould great bodies of workers into an organization, this principle of choosing the dominant factors for special attention and of lopping off the insignificant becomes a great principle of procedure.

In business this principle is more clearly recognized than it is in other activities, because business is self-supporting — it is one of the conditions of its life that it produces more than it consumes. It is a vital error here to exaggerate the insignificant or to slight the chief factors of existence. In other lines of endeavor, we may say, "This is a good thing to

THE LIMITS OF ORGANIZATION 35

do, I will do it"; but in industry, business, commerce, we say, "This seems a good thing to do; I will do it if it justifies the time, labor, thought, and sacrifice, — the cost of doing it; I will do it if the same time, labor, thought, and sacrifice will not accomplish something else that I can do that is better." The fact that business uses a standard of value by which to measure desirability, by which it can gauge the value of production and its cost, enables it to apply these principles of effective endeavor, but the particular standard of value that is used does not affect the principles, and they cannot be ignored when the standard is changed.

Many lines of endeavor have not at all money-value in view, — their ends are not at all material, — and yet, if their organization is to be effective, if it is to produce the best result for the expenditure of labor, time, and sacrifice, the cost by some standard of value must be counted, the ability of workers must be conserved; the same general principles of action apply as if the measurement were by the money-standard of value, — it makes no difference whether the direction of the endeavor is government of a people, the conversion of the heathen, the production of goods, scientific research, the winning of a game, or social regeneration.

The balancing of factors, the cutting out of the insignificant, analysis, judgment, and the choice of the " worth while," are not heroic accomplishments; they rather excite the impatience and contempt of those who are looking to the ends alone and will not count the cost. We are in a fair way to see the term "commercial," so much used in derogation and disparagement of the principles of business, gradually grow worse in its meaning, until it bears about the same relation to its original intent that "villain" does to "serf" or "peasant," and that "despot" does to "master." But, nevertheless, there is a true spirit of commerce, industry, and business, and these activities will continue to be of use to all branches of endeavor by the examples they furnish of choosing the essential and important and discarding the insignificant; and it is a principle that must be followed in any undertaking, or we end, after expending our resources, possessed of nothing worth having.

This may all seem a bit removed from the question of organization, but it really emphasizes something that organization does not tend to secure unless care is taken to preserve it. As business becomes organized and as duties become specialized, this question of cost does not always come home to each individual as it did when the individual had a hand in all questions and could see the bearing of all operations. The problem of organization bears a close resemblance to engineering problems. It requires analysis, it involves balancing and setting values, it is a constant estimation of the relation of parts to the whole, the function of these parts in the purpose of the whole, and we gain in setting about the problem with these ideas of proportion and relative value in our minds. It becomes one of the most important functions in the administration of an organization to preserve harmony and proper proportion in its workings, to provide for broad consideration of this question of cost and this question of " worth while," so that action will not be taken and work done simply because it is " good to do," regardless of the time, labor, thought, and sacrifice that it demands. The more we specialize to secure concentration of interest and economy in effort, the more carefully this must be watched, because the zeal of interested workers leads them to exaggerate the relative importance of their particular function. Each group of workers, each department in a business, is laboring at one component in the result, and the more zealous the leader of a group and the greater his ability, the more possibility there is that he may seek for results in his province that would not be justified if his factor were considered in relation to the whole purpose and result.

It is not an uncommon criticism of engineers and architects that they have a tendency to design the perfect structure, the one that all the most approved standards declare the best and that is the ideally suitable. The criticism is not devoid of basis because these men are specialists. It is not their province ordinarily to determine whether other factors in the whole result dictate a quality less than the perfect. Such questions, among others, as whether the structure is to be comparatively temporary or is to last fifty years, or whether the money necessary for construction can be raised on a four per cent basis or must be raised on a seven per cent basis, are questions for administrative officers to determine; and if they simply turn the structure design into an organization hopper, they run the risk that the zeal of the designer will exaggerate the relative importance of his function.

The national government has very greatly increased its functions in the last generation; and in this very large organization there are many specialists working hard and earnestly to turn out worthy products from their bureaus. But there is no necessity here that the value of the product exceed the cost. There is no "spirit of commercialism" to hold the course true to a definite end without meaningless excursions; and thus we see some elaborate products of the zeal of specialists that an administrative officer, considering the efficiency of his organization and with any standard of worth to work by, would have to cut out as "insignificant figures."

The street-railway organizations of many of the large cities have been furnishing in the last ten years an example of the danger of trusting to effective organizations for the extension and operation of the properties, without sufficient exercise by administrative officers of their function of preserving proportions and determining the relative importance of factors. The prices paid for the securities of street railways have been so greatly influenced by increasing gross earnings and economical operation, that the organizations have been stimulated to their greatest activity to secure growth and economy; and now the street railways begin to find that the desire for more business has saddled them with such long hauls and such onerous conditions, submitted to in order to secure growth, that it becomes a question whether the result is worth the time, labor, thought, and capital devoted to the undertakings.

In perfecting any business organization, we usually find parts that lag behind in effectiveness — that remain unsystematized even after others are carried to a high degree of refinement. It is an indication that one factor has been measured to a high degree of precision, and that there has been little more than guessing at another. This neglect of our "Precision of Measurement" principles is illustrated by the condition of the electric-lighting organizations some fifteen or twenty years ago. The dollars-and-cents accounting even at that time was pretty well systematized: other industries had developed principles of accounting that made possible the early adoption of a system well adapted to the electric lighting industry. Good systems were being introduced in the operation of the plants, the stations were better planned for economical working, they were weighing all coal, measuring and counting all supplies, establishing stock-rooms, systematizing inspection, repairs, and construction; but there was a curious anomaly in the organizations. Those carrying on the electric-lighting business had considered it a business of supplying light and not of supplying electrical energy. All the companies were counting pretty accurately the cost of operating their plants, and yet very few of them had any means of measuring the thing they produced and were selling. When it was a question of accounting for every cent that came into the company, or that was paid out, the system was perfect; but when it came to knowing what was produced, how many kilowatt hours of electrical energy went out over the wires, there was no system at all. These were organizations in the process of forming, and it shows well the possibility there always is of neglecting entirely an important factor in a result. Happily the electric-light companies are now almost universally provided with meters that measure every kilowatt hour of output, and a unit is secured by which all items of income and expenditure may be judged. With a zeal, however, that is perhaps born of the delay in securing this new facility, we sometimes now see lighting men breaking another rule for efficient endeavor by magnifying the insignificant, and calculating kilowatt-hour costs for every item they can discover.

The ambition of men to make their establishments great and inclusive, the desire for a complete organization, leads sometimes to its extension into unwarranted fields. The successful shop comes to grief as a department store too small to gain the advantages of specialization; and the factory proving its usefulness in a limited field is carried down because a foundry to supply its castings or a wood-working shop to supply other parts seems to add to the completeness of the organization, but is not justified by the size of the business. It might seem to improve and complete a construction organization, for instance, to add to its force inspectors of material, who would watch manufacture and test the product; and yet such a move might be wasteful and accomplish comparatively poor results, if it were possible to employ for this purpose a firm who did much inspecting and testing, and that alone. It is always a pleasure to see a thing run like "clock-work," but it is not always safe to use this quality as a criterion of value, because an organization may run like "clock-work" and yet accomplish poor results with great waste. There is such a thing as over-organization, excess of systematization, excess of division for specialization. Dividing out a function that is independent of other activities simplifies, gives definiteness to the plan, places responsibility more accurately, and increases the product of effort through specialization; but when we attempt divisions that are too fine, when we get to dividing functions that are not naturally independent, we weaken the connection of the activities with the nerve centre that coördinates, and we increase greatly the difficulty of coöperation. If we attempt to make duties independent that are not naturally independent, we may get two departments attempting to do the same thing, or, in their effort to avoid the friction and confusion resulting from this, they both avoid the duties about which there is question and matters fall between them unattended to. This forced independence results in duplication of work. To maintain independence, each of several groups sometimes provides for facilities that could easily serve all groups. Thus organization carried along wrong lines, though it seems an extension to the structure, may in reality have the same result as no organization. The National Government unfortunately furnishes examples of this. The recent discussion of the reorganization of the Navy Department has brought out the waste and lack of harmony that come from the separation into bureaus that are forced to be too independent, and that are without means for the coördination that must exist in effective administration. Keeping to the old divisions made for the purpose of control and the fixing of responsibility, the department has been left with no one responsible for the coördination of the bureaus and for the elimination of the duplication of plant and work. The simple dividing up and separating of complex duties brings one kind of order, but it is not a very high form of organization, because it can usually be only temporarily effective. A change in conditions may make the division a wrong one, and the arising of relations between the divisions puts too much strain on pure coöperation. Moreover, these very definite divisions often leave the same kind of work to be performed by many different departments, and all advantage in concentrating and systematizing a particular branch of work is lost. There necessarily arises in this way much duplication in facilities and in work. It is probably too much to expect coördination not only between the bureaus of the same government department, but also between different departments. An amusing illustration of the independence of the different government departments is the experience recently of a Boston business house. The Census Bureau requires of this house each year rather elaborate returns regarding its business. They are prepared with care and are on file in the Census office. There appeared one day a man from the Department of Justice; he wished certain information about the business, but was told that it was too bad he had come all the way to Boston for it, because exactly that information was on file in the Census office in the very form he wished it. But, said he, "We haven't anything to do with the Census Bureau; that is in another department." By a curious coincidence, while the Department of Justice man was in the office a letter was received from the Department of Commerce and Labor, which wished the same information about the business. "This is easily arranged," said the business house to the Department of Justice man: "we will simply write the Department of Commerce and Labor to see you; that we have just given you all the information." "Don't do that," said the Department of Justice man. "He couldn't get anything from me. The departments are separate."

It is safe to say that those responsible for any established business or industry have constantly to be on their guard against the continuance of outgrown systems and against the gradual adding of detail to an old method for the purpose of meeting new conditions, when a new and simpler method would be far more efficient. It is one of the benefits of organization that it provides established ways of doing things; but there is an element of weakness in this very advantage, if we grow to look upon the established order as inviolable because of custom and long use. This is conspicuous in the "red tape" that results from perfunctory approval. Wherever there are systematic ways of doing things, checks are used to guard against errors of judgment, neglect, or carelessness, and as several persons may be required to catch all possible errors, it may be necessary that letters, papers, material, or work pass through several hands to receive approval. One may note at times in just such procedure the hanging on to an outgrown system by the requirement of this inspection and approval that has long before lost its significance. It is the force of habit in organization, the discipline that holds to established methods. Accounting, records, and statistics help us in discovering the useless and ineffective, but these detecting agencies rarely turn against themselves, and we have need of caution here also to see that analysis does

THE LIMITS OF ORGANIZATION

not become directed to the non-essential, and that we are not recording facts of little moment. We sometimes get over-organization that results in doing more than is necessary, following out work to greater refinement than is worth while. This is sometimes true in the determination of costs. The attempt to keep close watch over all wastes sometimes results in a system for the purpose so elaborate that the cost of the system itself becomes an important factor. While it pays to know costs, it also pays to find out how much it costs to know costs.

But though we find elements of weakness in the very process of organization, they are not weaknesses that necessarily grow greater with the size of the structure. The limits are not limits that come only with size. With the growth of the structure comes still further division into groups and greater need of coördinating ability in administrative officers, but there remain always the same underlying principles of efficient endeavor: the choosing of the things worth doing, the emphasizing of factors that have the greatest bearing on the result, and the elimination of that which has no significance. It is true that in the end we have to say that this choosing and this judgment is the important matter, but we must realize that it is not to be supposed that organization will take the place of business ability. Organization is but a means to an end; it provides a method. It can never take the place of business judgment, or intuitive sense of what is wise to do, or vigorous initiative that sets things in motion ; but it can help to secure these by relieving from detail those who must exercise the judgment, and by bringing to them the premises they need; and it can help the execution by providing orderly procedure for carrying out the action that is determined upon.

THE ORGANIZATION OF ADMINISTRATION

WHEN able and effective business administration is mentioned, probably to most of us there comes to mind the kind of man that for so long has been the type of the efficient business administrator, the figure that in so many industries has stood in the commanding position, knowing all details at first-hand. He is the man who owns and administers his undertaking. He has been the conceiver of the purpose, the one who has seen all branches of the business develop; who knows the bearings of all factors; who, in lieu of a system for securing discipline, has perhaps subjected himself to discipline and furnished an example of strict and systematic attention to business in his own adherence to routine; who, as the creator of the processes, the administrator of each part, the builder of the structure, is of unquestioned superiority and the one with supreme authority.

There is good reason why such a man represents to us efficient administration. As long as the business that he administers is within his range and has not grown in size beyond his grasp and ability to control and direct in detail, he is able, by himself, to be the means of securing the benefits of many of the factors that we have found are necessary in constructing an effective organization. There is no indefiniteness as regards authority and responsibility, because they rest in him except as he delegates them specifically, and, as far as administration alone goes, he is sure of *esprit de corps*, coöperation, and "team play," because the units to be harmonized are already one.

This type of man is passing, however, to some extent. The type of organization that he presided over and the type of administration by means of which he presided have been largely superseded, because large size has secured advantages and brought economies that exceed the benefits that can be derived from the superior executive power of the older type of administration. Moreover, the increasing size of industries and various business undertakings has brought the necessity of organizing the contribution of capital. The business corporation has come into being, by means of which great numbers may join in furnishing capital for the carrying out of undertakings.

Many or even all of these contributors may be ignorant of the business they have invested in. They intrust their contributions to those representing the corporation, and the statutes authorizing the forming of these corporations have had to specify somewhat the form the organization shall take, because of the necessity of protecting the individuals who contribute the capital, and also those who may become the creditors of the whole body. There thus immediately become introduced into undertakings carried on by corporations, factors in the administration that did not exist when one man owned his business and directed it. Authority and responsibility are to some extent forced into definite places. The law provides that there shall be a body of directors who represent the owners and are responsible to them for the proper conduct of the business. It provides that there shall be a president as the head executive authority, that there shall be a treasurer who is responsible for the proper use of the funds, that there shall be a secretary who shall record the acts of the directors. Here begin to arise many of the difficulties of corporations, because the law specifies the form of organization necessary for protection, and this form is not always the one that would be chosen with regard only to the effective carrying out of the purposes of the organization.

In the theory of corporation administration, the owners are to delegate to certain of their number the responsibility of directing the affairs of the company, of deciding upon the officers who are to manage the affairs, and of passing upon the acts of these officers. Five or six men, joining together in corporate form to develop an enterprise or carry on a business, find the process comparatively simple. They give their time, attention, and judgment to all matters, and if the interest of each in this enterprise bears a large proportion to his total interests, and they all have expert knowledge of the undertaking, the affairs may be nearly or quite as well handled as the affairs of the partnership or of the individual. When, however, the number of stockholders becomes hundreds or thousands, an entirely different condition exists. The government of the corporation becomes a representative government, with a probability either of unequal representation by dominant men, or of representation by men not familiar with the property or business, nor free to give the time necessary to know sufficient detail for wise and independent judgment. Ten or twelve representatives acting together cannot give effective administration. Numbers are good for conference, to protect against prejudice and against warps and twists, to bring out by discussion all relevant factors, to throw upon problems side-lights from varied experience, and to assure regular procedure; but the autocrat's command is superior in effectiveness. It saves time, and permits quick action upon conclusions formed, but not formulated. There is much denunciation of corporation autocrats, but it is probable that the dominance of single strong men in corporations is much less due to a desire for selfish advantage, than to the impatience of vigorous executives over the delay necessitated in presenting questions with full and orderly exposition to bodies of men, and in bringing them to a conclusion by discussion and argument.

But whether it seems best from the point of view of effective administration or not, we shall undoubtedly have to consider in an increasing degree the presentation of information to boards of directors, and to some extent to representatives of the public as well. It is a factor that must be reckoned with in the organization of the administration of corporations. The corporation's capital is contributed by many people, the work of the corporation is carried on by great numbers whose lot in life is cast with the project, the product of the corporation's activities becomes in many cases essential to the well-being of those it serves, and it will hardly be permitted that the integrity of such enterprises shall rest upon the rise or fall, upon the wisdom or foolishness or honesty, of one man. The results become too far-reaching to be dependent upon the life and health of one man, however able and honest; and whatever may seemingly be gained in this way temporarily, through vigorous and able direction, is more than offset by the instability or uncertainty of the corporate affairs. Organizations are thus having brought to them a new problem; they have to provide stability in administration as well as efficiency, to preserve the vigor of initiative of the individual, and yet to benefit by the judgment of many, and they have to assure the continuity in administration that is demanded by the span of life of the corporation, and the increasing time necessary to earn enough to return with interest the capital contributed to the undertaking.

These needs are not inconsistent with good organization and efficient administration. The mere size and complexity of modern undertakings necessitate for the information of administrators much of the system for gathering facts and for their orderly presentation that is necessary in acquainting representatives of stockholders or public with the essentials of the business. These corporate needs and the great size of undertakings do, however, require that administration be organized with the same care that is given to the productive processes themselves. It becomes impossible, as in old-time business, that administrators shall have intimate and expert knowledge of all details and all processes. If they attempt to gather this at first-hand, they arrive in administrative positions at an age when they no longer have the vigorous initiative of youth with which to attack administrative problems, and some of their detail knowledge is already antiquated and inapplicable.

In some cases, it becomes necessary to treat administration almost as a function in itself; to choose administrators for their power of initiation, for their sense of proportion, for their ability to pick the essential, and to supplement them with organization that brings to them the conclusions of the expert in the finer detail of the parts. The mechanism through which the administrative officers gather their knowledge about the progress and the working of the organization, and the means by which they coördinate the parts and carry out their policy of procedure, vary with the plan on which the structure is built.

There is always the question, in organizations, of the relative importance of subdividing into parts having the same general characteristics as the whole, and subdividing into parts involving one function. This has been mentioned before, but it is worth while for illustration to apply the two forms to the same case. If, for example, one were to organize the feeding of a community, and should go to the extreme in subdividing into parts similar to the whole, he would divide into households or families, placing each in the care of one person, who would be responsible for everything in connection with the feeding of his household, buying food of all kinds, cooking this food, serving it, and disposing of the waste. These families would be grouped into districts, and subordinate officers would have charge of these groups. It would be an organization similar to a part of the military organization, where the captain commands the company as a part of the regiment commanded by the colonel. If one should go to the extreme in subdividing according to functions, he would attempt to gather his community into one or more centres for meals. He would divide the functions so that buying would form one department, cooking another, serving another, and disposing of waste another. He might even subdivide these functions.

It is clear that the first method tends to facility of direction and control, and has no limits to its applicability; new families and new groups of families could be added without introducing confusion or overloading administrative offices. However bad and wasteful the feeding may be, no widespread difficulties can arise; each unit is independent, and responsibility can be definitely and quickly placed. There are no large problems of coördination, and the quality of the service will vary with the individuals having charge of the different households. The functional organization will be more complex, but it brings into play division of labor and the conserving of special skill. The systematic purchasing by a department that does nothing but purchase, will result in better food for the same expenditure. It will be possible to have cooking that is better and more uniform. It is conceivable that the economies from wise purchasing, the division of labor, and the saving of waste, might result in very great saving, or in very superior service for the same cost as by the first method of organization. But this functional organization would have its difficulties. There would be trouble in coördinating the duties of the different departments. The Cooking Department would disagree with the Purchasing Department about the quality of the food, the Cooking and the Serving Departments would have their disagreements as to the quality of the cooking, and the way the food was delivered to the servers. Mistakes or catastrophes or inability in one department would seriously affect the whole result, because the parts would be interdependent. Responsibility for results as a whole would be difficult to place. The establishment would require great skill and ability in administration. It would be in unstable equilibrium, and would not automatically, and without skillful direction, give even a fair degree of service.

One can easily imagine many combinations of these two methods. The purchasing might be done for all, and yet the households remain independent. The whole community might be divided into half a dozen units, each of which was functionally organized. There might be many independent units, with advisory boards divided according to functions.

Most organizations really combine the two principles, and as affecting administration, the important question is the extent to which functional organization shall be carried. It is broadly true that, as one divides into independent subdivisions, instead of by functions, the grasp of situations as a whole is strengthened, there is greater ease of coördination, the facility of control and direction is increased; and it is also broadly true that as one divides according to functions, economy of effort and quality of work are secured. The extent to which functional organization is carried in the administrative organization varies greatly with different businesses, because there is a great difference in the degree to which the different functions are interwoven and interdependent. The loss on account of difficulties of coördination sometimes more than counterbalances any advantage from economy that can come from functional division. One commonly finds the more plainly independent functions separated. In industrial companies it is usual to find an administrative officer in charge of production, another in charge of financial matters and accounting, another in charge of selling. These are likely to be pretty independent functions, and such coördination as is necessary can usually be secured by meetings of the different subheads with the head of the organization. Such an organization appears to be completely functional, and if it is not large, it may be considered so. But imagine it very large. We immediately meet most of the problems over again. Production, for instance, has been set off as a functional department, but when we begin to get great size, we have again to consider an extension and elaboration of the organization. Shall we subdivide the broad function of production into minor functions, separating processes or duties; or shall we subdivide into separate plants, each, so far as production goes, an independent unit?

Many of the telephone companies have recently, it is understood, reorganized on the functional basis. A general manager is at the head of the operating organization; under him are three administrative officers, one of whom has general charge of all selling of telephone service, all relations with the subscribers and public. A second administrative officer has general charge of the operation of the exchanges and other plants. His province is to provide the service. The third administrative officer has general charge of the construction and maintenance of plants. He must provide the means for giving service. These three officers are at the head of their functions over the whole territory. This territory is subdivided into divisions, and in each division there are three functional heads corresponding to the general heads. The divisions are further divided into districts, so that even in one city there may be these three men on the same level as to rank, but with different functions for which they are responsible and over which they are in authority.

One can assume with some assurance where the advantages and where the difficulties in such an organization lie, but no one, of course, except the telephone people, is qualified to judge the relative importance of these advantages and difficulties. It is safe to say that business-getting will be much more effectively carried on, that operation and the giving of service will be of better quality and show better efficiency of effort, that plants will be better built and better cared for at lower cost. The concentration of effort, the conserving of special skill, the coördination and coöperation within each functional division, will all help in perfecting each function as a thing in itself. On the other hand, one will naturally look for difficulties in coördinating the different functions. Serious differences of opinion on questions involving all three functions, unless the superior functional heads agree, will have to travel up to the general manager before a crossing point is reached; before any one is found with authority in all the three divisions of the business.

In many businesses this would be an insuperable difficulty. Probably, in the early days of the telephone it would have caused too much confusion to be warranted by advantages in other ways. The telephone business has now become established on a definite basis. Its plant is more nearly standardized and its methods are more nearly fixed. The sections of the telephone system are not so much independent plants as they were, and there is not the same proportional creation of new telephone territory. If the business were nearer the time of its formation, when franchises in different places had to be secured, when the securing of subscribers, the nature of the service, and the extension of plant into new sections, all became parts of larger questions and were intimately interwoven, it is quite likely that grasp of the situation as a whole would seem, as it apparently did seem, of first importance, and would dictate a type of organization that provided for at least one in authority for each section.

Such an organization as the telephone companies have adopted seeks to provide the chief administrative officer in the operating department with an effective advisory board of three members. They cover the three branches of the business, and come to the general manager with expert knowledge of these branches, and with the records, statistics, and conclusions that their own departments have compiled. They have had experience in conference. They have argued out and settled between themselves many questions involving the three functions, that have not come to the general manager. If three men must agree, there is assurance against unwise action, and a larger number of questions are left for them to decide. The chief administrator may be chosen for his qualities as an administrator rather than for his detailed knowledge of the functions. He may be chosen for his skill in coördinating, in weighing the importance of factors, in discounting the narrower view of the specialist, in initiating new or better policies. All essential factors necessary for decision and for initiative come to him in systematic form. He is relieved from detail and can consider matters broadly. His own knowledge is in the form to pass on to directors, and thus to meet the provisions of the law's requirements for corporations. The directors may not direct in the sense of taking the initiative, but this operating executive is in a position to prove to the president and to the directors that his proposed initiative is right. He may not be the autocratic dictator, but it is in his power to gain much of the effectiveness in administration that the dictator gains, because if his conclusions are right, he has every advantage in presenting them with convincing force to the checking body that the law requires.

These things are necessary in effective administration, but they have sometimes to be secured by a different type of organization. The organization that Stone & Webster have built up for the administration of the affairs of public service corporations is interesting in this connection because it is an organization purely for administration and management, and the administrative problems stand out more clearly than when they appear more closely connected with the operating and producing parts of an organization. It would not be found applicable in all administration. It takes its form because of its purposes and necessities, but a consideration of it will indicate some of the problems that all administrative organizations have to meet.

The Stone & Webster management organization is a separate corporate body. It is not administering a single corporation, but thirty or forty. The activities of these corporations are not in one city, or one state, or one country. They not only operate in separate places, but with two or three exceptions, one corporation has no relation whatever with another. Each is a distinct corporate entity, with its own list of stockholders, its own board of directors, and its own funds; but the administration is the same in all cases. The management organization chooses the local manager for each company and the local assistant treasurer, who has charge of local accounts and funds. It directs the local manager, and instructs the assistant treasurer and audits his accounts. It decides upon plant and equipment, does much of the larger purchasing, directs the policy of the companies. The officers of the companies are chosen largely from the administrative officers of the organization. It places the companies' loans, it decides upon advisable extensions, and it negotiates the sales of securities for providing fresh capital. It must do these things with the approval of the boards of directors, and must carry out in all the thirty or forty companies the legal procedure that the statutes require. It is conceivable that such a managing organization could be set up after a functional plan; that the operation of the properties should be one department, the choice and construction and maintenance of the plants another, the relations with the public and the securing of business another, and the financial affairs another; and at the head an executive who would coördinate all, bridge the gaps, and take the comprehensive view of the whole.

There are many reasons why this is impracticable. The companies are not subject to the same operating conditions. Their equipment is not and cannot well be standard. The state laws to which they are subject differ. The procedure for the raising of money differs. The rates at which they can attract new capital differ widely. The local feeling toward corporations is different, and the public demands that the companies must meet are by no means the same. Constant coördination is necessary between financial questions and construction questions, between financial questions and operating questions, between the getting of business and the providing of plant.

Local questions, territorial questions, the companies' attitude and policy, the broad view of their affairs as a whole, need constantly to be considered. Whatever economy might be secured from a functional plan in the managing organization would be wiped out by the losses from failure to coördinate, from the weakening of a company's position by the less comprehensive and less strong grasp of its affairs as a whole.

The type of organization that has proved to be the best in this case is one for firmer grasp and fuller knowledge of each local situation as a complete situation and problem in itself. The local operating organizations, which we are not at the moment considering, are largely functional. The administration organization begins with the local manager, who is at the head of all local affairs. The thirty or forty companies managed by the administration organization are grouped into six territorial divisions. All the managers in one of these divisions or districts are directly responsible to a district manager, who is broadly and directly responsible for local company operation, upkeep, and development, including relations with the public. There remain many questions in the administration of corporations of this kind. There are negotiations in connection with the purchase of properties to be consolidated, a great number of questions regarding corporate organization, reorganization, relations of holding companies, the securing of charters, conferences with attorneys regarding corporate acts, the holding of directors' meetings, and the preparation of matter to be presented at these meetings, the preparation of financial plans, and the carrying out of these plans when approved by company directors, and the issue and sale of securities.

These are Boston affairs. They must be cared for in Boston, where much of the money has to be raised for fresh capital, and where the directors of the companies live and meet. They are matters a step beyond the district managers, and are attended to by three vice-presidents of the administration organization, each of whom is at the head of the companies in two districts. At the head of the organization is a president, who harmonizes policies and initiates modifications, who consults with the vice-presidents, who coördinates, and who rules any border-land of indefinite responsibility.

The board of directors of this management organization is composed of the leading men in the organization, and it meets once a week to confer on questions of policy, to discuss questions that will be helped toward a solution by the combined judgment and varied abilities and points of view of the men at the top. They together approve the choice of managers; they decide upon changes in organization and upon standard procedure. From their number, and sometimes with the addition of experts, they form committees for the threshing out of problems that affect all companies. It is a body of discussion and conference.

64 THE ORGANIZATION OF ADMINISTRATION

There are many things that this administration organization does that are in the nature of functions, and there are functional departments, but they do not affect the general plan of the structure or interfere with the lines of authority and placing of responsibility. The organization is planned to give, above all, broad grasp of the local companies, direct control, and effective direction. The functional departments in this case are auxiliaries. They are assistants. They separate out duties that an administrator would perform himself if he had the time, and the special knowledge and facility; if attention to these duties would not distract him from more important matters in his broad supervision; and if it did not save great duplication and waste to have them performed for several administrators by the same force of men and the same equipment.

These functional departments instruct the local offices in regard to the keeping of local books, audit the companies' books and vouchers, file company documents, see that properties are properly protected by insurance, compile and compare statistics of operation and costs, decide upon suitable plant and equipment, make the larger purchases where combined orders are an advantage, negotiate loans and sales of securities, prepare statements and reports to stockholders, prepare financial statements and information for officers and directors, and prepare systematically matter for directors to act upon, consult company attorneys and assure that all votes are in proper form and all corporate acts legally carried out, keep calendars of all corporate events so that no necessary action will be forgotten; and one of these departments keeps records too of the men in the organization who will be eligible for promotion, the kind of ability they have, the quality of the work they have been doing, and the reports about them or about their work by their superiors.

There are heads to the different departments who are responsible for the work done there, and the functions are important; but the administrative organization could not be built up about these departments, because their work is on the detail of the administrative work. They are simply to assist the administrators to see that accounts are accurate accounts, that figures represent truly the conditions, that information is properly analyzed and presented for the formations of conclusions, and when conclusions are reached, to determine what procedure must be followed, to take all detail steps, and to assure also that there is coming along always a supply of men who are qualifying for executive positions. These departments do the things that the administrator of a single company is likely to do in his own office, well or ill, according to his particular bent or prejudices. Within these departments duties may be definitely assigned, and there is definiteness in the division of duties between departments, but there is no difficulty in the fact that three vice-presidents have authority over these departments, because the work they do for these different officers is distinct. It has to do with different companies and different territories.

This organization for its particular problem gives in this way its solution for the modern needs in administration. It preserves in a single head the control and broad grasp of a company's affairs, fixes the responsibility, and thus preserves initiative and vigor of action. It relieves this head from detail, and leaves him free for the exercise of the judgment and executive ability for which he is chosen. It provides for conference and discussion to eliminate prejudices and twists, to help coördinate where it is necessary, and to bring out all factors to be considered. It provides machinery for bringing to the boards of directors all pertinent information, all premises and deductions and plans for action. It assures that all the checks and safeguards provided by law are respected, that all legal regulations are followed. It attempts to provide a continuing stream of skill and ability working along through the activities of the organization, so that the well-being of the companies will not rest on the life and health of an individual.

It has been plain in this consideration of different plans for the division of work and responsibility that, when we talk about functional organization and organization for broad grasp and control, we are not discussing two radically different types, two "schools" of organization. We are only discussing the advisable bounds of duties. These bounds are sometimes drawn about territories or about parts that are simi-

THE ORGANIZATION OF ADMINISTRATION

lar to the whole in their structure; sometimes they are drawn about functions that are a part of the whole. Whether, for effective administration, it is best to draw these bounds in one way or the other, depends upon the independence of what we include in a group. All social activities are divided into functions. We discuss the organization of a railroad, and yet the business of a railroad is but one of the functions of modern society. In its organization, the operation is set off as a distinct part or group of duties, and this is done because this function is largely independent. It is less interwoven with traffic affairs, for instance, than the whole of the railroad business in one territory is interwoven with the whole of the railroad business in adjoining territory. When the reverse is true, and territories become the more independent factors, the organization of the railroad changes.

In the Stone & Webster management organization we have seen that territories were the independent factors and dictated the plan of the organization. Yet this management of properties is but a function in the whole organization of the firm of Stone & Webster, because this comprises also a construction business and a banking business. In the plan of the whole business, the parts that are most independent have been most definitely set off; and in these parts that have been set off, the smaller parts, around which bounds could be drawn, have formed the main elements of the structure of the minor organizations.

The time that one man can devote to a duty is limited, and his capacity is limited. It is no longer possible for the head of a great organization to know all the detail of an undertaking, or even to know of all the minor coördination. He can be directly responsible for but little of the actual action, but he must know when the action goes wrong. He must know the result toward which action is tending. He is responsible for the result. His province is to initiate, to set activities in motion, to keep the sense of proportion, to recognize the essential, to coördinate the activities. But as in the administrative system of our own bodies, he, the mind of the organization, must leave to lower ganglia, to lower nerve centres, the minor coördinations. He is the cerebrum and must care for the higher coördinations. He must know all that goes on in the organization, but it must not take his time and attention to secure the knowledge. He must be provided with information, analyzed, sifted, and compiled, ready for the application of his judgment. He must initiate new policies, new kinds of action, but he must be provided with a working system that responds to his initiative.

The administrative officers are in this way in position to present to the directing body required of corporations by the statutes, conclusions systematized and fortified and definite in their plan. The directors may remain the safeguard they were in theory to be, but if the administrative officers are effective, the administration of the corporation is effective.